Sacred Sites
of Center City

A guide to Philadelphia's historic churches, synagogues and meetinghouses

A publication of the Preservation Alliance for Greater Philadelphia

John Andrew Gallery, Project Director and General Editor

Photographs by Tom Crane

pdb PAUL DRY BOOKS, INC.
Philadelphia 2007

Old City

The first permanent settlement in Philadelphia was located between Vine and Walnut Streets, from Front to 4th streets. Within this compact area were houses, shops, public markets, and schools, as well as numerous religious buildings. Second and Market streets was the heart of the city and the location of the Greater Quaker Meetinghouse and the principal Anglican church.

As the residential population gradually moved south and west in the 19th century, commercial and industrial buildings of varying architectural styles replaced the colonial houses. Old City was rediscovered in the 1980s when it was designated a National Register Historic District. This led to the conversion of commercial loft buildings to residential use and contributed to the creation of a vibrant neighborhood with numerous art galleries, restaurants, and distinctive shops. This rich history surrounds some of the oldest and most historic religious properties in Philadelphia.

The walking tour of sacred sites in Old City begins at 2nd and Market streets.

Christ Church (Episcopal)

2nd Street, between Market and Arch streets

1727-44, Dr. John Kearsley, supervisor
1751-54, steeple, Robert Smith

Services: Sunday: 9am, 11am; Wednesday, 12pm

Also open: Monday – Saturday: 9am – 5pm; Sunday: 1 – 5pm

Closed major holidays and on Monday and Tuesday in January and February

215-922-1695—www.christchurchphila.org

William Penn's charter from the king specified that Anglican ministers could settle freely in Pennsylvania. They arrived early, established a church at 2nd and Market streets in 1695 and constructed a wooden chapel there in 1697. When the new church was built, it was modeled after the work of British architect Sir Christopher Wren, who rebuilt many of the churches in London after the Great Fire. In the colonial era, Benjamin Franklin, George Washington, Betsy Ross and some members of Penn's family worshipped here; their pews are marked with commemorative plaques. After the Revolution, a new denomination, the Protestant Episcopal Church in the United States, was founded here.

Christ Church is a National Historic Landmark and a superb example of Georgian architecture. It is distinguished by high-relief exterior details including projecting cornices, arches, quoins, round-arched windows and a balustrade hiding the roof. On the east wall, a large Palladian window provides light for the chancel. The 200-foot steeple, financed by lotteries sponsored by Benjamin Franklin, was the tallest structure in North America for nearly 100 years.

While the church appears to have changed little since its construction, the interior has been remodeled several times and was most recently restored in the 1980s.

Arch Street Meetinghouse

Arch Street, between 3rd and 4th streets

1803-11, Owen Biddle, architect
1968, addition, Cope and Lippincott
Services: Sunday: 10:30am; Wednesday: 7pm
Also open: Monday – Saturday: 10am – 4pm
215-627-2667—www.archstreetfriends.org

William Penn and many early settlers of
Pennsylvania were members of the Religious
Society of Friends (Quakers). Penn gave this
site to the Quaker community in 1701 for
use as a burial ground. When the Great
Meetinghouse at 2nd and Market streets
could no longer accommodate the Yearly
Meetings when men and women met sepa-
rately for business, this new meetinghouse
was constructed. It was first occupied by the
Women's Yearly Meeting in the east wing,
then joined by the Men's Yearly Meeting
when the west wing was completed.

Arch Street Meetinghouse is the second
oldest and largest meetinghouse in the city.
The plain brick structure with simple porti-
cos over the doorways reflects Friends' rejec-
tion of ornamentation and symbolism. The
west wing retains its original character, with
plain wood floors and wooden benches. The
east wing contains dioramas depicting high-
lights of William Penn's career and other
changing exhibits.

The meetinghouse is the home of the
Monthly Meeting of Friends of Philadelphia,
which worships here weekly. The annual
sessions of Philadelphia Yearly Meeting are
held here in March. The meetinghouse
frequently hosts gatherings and conferences
of organizations active in work for peace
and social justice.

Old First Reformed Church, United Church of Christ

4th and Race streets

1837, Andrew D. Caldwell, builder
1976, restored, Paul Richard Frantz, architect
Services: Sunday: 11am

Also open: Monday – Friday: 8am – 2pm
*Inquire at church office, 151 North Fourth
Street or by telephone.*
215-922-4566—www.oldfirstucc.org

Old First Reformed Church was founded by
a German congregation in 1727. As the
congregation grew, a second church was built
on the site, followed by the current church in
1837. However, by the 1880s the neighborhood consisted primarily of commercial
businesses and warehouses. The congregation
moved to North and then West Philadelphia,
and the church became a paint manufacturing company and warehouse.

In 1967, the congregation learned that its
former neighborhood was to be revitalized
and that the old church building was for sale.
The group voted to return to the original
location and began a 10-year process of
restoring the church. The plain exterior brick
structure houses a large light-filled sanctuary
on the second floor, which contains the original altar surround discovered behind the
partitions of the paint warehouse.

Old First Reformed Church has an active
social ministry; it holds a summer day camp
in North Philadelphia, hosts concerts and
community meetings, a winter homeless
shelter, a weekly food cupboard, work camps
for youth from around the country and a
live-animal crèche at Christmas.

Old St. George's United Methodist Church

4th Street, between Race and Vine streets at New Street

1763-69, attributed to Robert Smith
Altered 1804, 1836

Services: Sunday: 11am;
summer—Sunday: 10am

Also open: 10am – 4pm. Ring bell on New Street.

215-925-7788—www.historicstgeorges.org

St. George's is the oldest Methodist church in continuous use in the country. The property was purchased from a German Calvinist congregation, which could not afford to complete the church it had commissioned in 1763. During the colonial period, St. George's was home to several important preachers including Francis Asbury, deemed first Bishop of American Methodism and Richard Allen, the first licensed African American Methodist preacher and founder of the African Methodist Episcopal Church. In 1921, St. George's became known as "the church that moved the bridge." When it was proposed that the church be moved for construction of the Benjamin Franklin Bridge, the courts ruled that the bridge be moved in order to save the church.

St. George's has a plain facade and little decorative ornament. The intimate interior is full of light, thanks to the large, clear, multi-paned windows. It contains a three-sided gallery and white-painted, paneled pews. Adjacent to the church is the Museum of American Methodism, which includes the Francis Asbury Bible and the John Wesley Chalice Cup, as well as other Methodist memorabilia and a research library.

St. Augustine's Roman Catholic Church

4th Street, between Race and Vine Streets at New Street

1847-48, Napoleon LeBrun
1867-72, tower and steeple, Edwin Durang
Altered 1895, 1923

Services: Saturday: 5:15pm; Sunday: 9am – 11am, 7pm; Monday – Friday: 12:05pm

Also open: Inquire by phone.

215-627-1838—www.st-augustinechurch.com

St. Augustine's was founded in 1796 by Augustinian friars and a church completed in 1824 to provide a place of worship for Catholics in the area then known as Northern Liberties. Although Pennsylvania offered religious freedom to Roman Catholics, there was still much prejudice. During anti-Catholic riots in 1844, St. Augustine's was burned by rioters who resented its Irish-immigrant congregation.

The present church was designed by the Catholics' favorite architect of that era, Napoleon LeBrun. He combined the Georgian-style plan of the earlier building with Renaissance-inspired details, such as the facade's Doric pediment and the round-arched windows. The ornate interior includes late-19th-century paintings by Filippo Costaggini and ceiling frescoes by Nicola Monachesi, contributing to the church's neo-Baroque feel. The tower's octagonal spire and domed top, dismantled in 1992 after suffering damage in a hurricane-force storm, was recreated in 1995.

St. Augustine's has become a multi-cultural congregation as a result of its being named the American Shrine for Santo Niño de Cebu (The Holy Child) in 1991. This made the church the center of the large Filipino community in the Philadelphia area.

Free Quaker Meetinghouse

5th and Arch streets
1783-85, Samuel Wetherill, builder
1868, Stephen D. Button
1961-69 restoration, F. Spencer Roach
Not currently in religious use.

*Open: Memorial Day to Labor Day:
9am – 5pm; Labor Day to Memorial Day:
Wednesday – Sunday: 10am – 4pm*

215-629-5801 x 202

Members of the Religious Society of Friends (Quakers) were pacifists, and individuals who actively participated in the American Revolution were expelled from their meetings. Carpenter/builder Sam Wetherill led a group of these "fighting" Quakers to build this meetinghouse, which continued to host Quaker meetings until 1834.

From the exterior, it appears that the structure rejects the Quaker plain style in favor of a sophisticated design that includes red and black glazed brick, a dentil cornice and pedimented entrance. However, the brightly lit interior is more austere, with traditional wood benches and a small gallery. The basement once incorporated storage vaults located under the street that were rented for income. These vaults were destroyed in 1961, when the structure was moved to its current site and restored by the Junior League of Philadelphia.

Today, the meetinghouse is owned and managed by the National Park Service. An interpretative program is offered in the meetinghouse during the summer months.

Congregation Mikveh Israel and the National Museum of American Jewish History

4th Street, between Arch and Market streets
1976, H2L2 Architects
*Services: Monday–Friday: 7:15am, 8pm;
Saturday: 9am, 7:30pm; Sunday: 8:15am*

215-922-5446—www.mikvehisrael.org

*Museum Open: Monday – Thursday: 10am –
5pm; Friday: 10am – 3pm; Sunday: 12 – 5pm*

215-923-3811—www.nmajh.org

Congregation Mikveh Isreal was founded in 1740 when Nathan Levy purchased a plot of land near 8th and Spruce streets for a burial ground. It is the oldest Jewish congregation in Philadelphia and the second oldest in the nation. Among its early members were Revolutionary War financiers Haym Solomon and Isaac Moses. The congregation's first building, located near 4th and Cherry streets in 1782, was replaced by a larger building designed by William Strickland in 1825, then by another designed by John McArthur, Jr., in 1860. In 1909, the congregation moved to North Philadelphia to find a larger site, and then moved to its current location in 1976.

The congregation worships in the Sephardic, Spanish/Portuguese tradition introduced by Reverend Gerhsom Menes Sexias in 1780. The worship space contains artifacts from earlier synagogues.

The associated National Museum of American Jewish History is the only museum of its kind in the country. Since 1976, the museum has provided visitors the opportunity to learn about the history of the participation of American Jews in the social, cultural, economic and political life of the nation. It features permanent and changing exhibits, educational programs and a collection of more than 7,500 objects.

Society Hill

A s Old City became more congested, affluent families moved south into the area now known as Society Hill. In the colonial period, Society Hill contained the homes of the wealthy and the poor, markets, taverns and notable churches. Today Society Hill contains the largest concentration of original 18th-century architecture of any place in the United States.

As the city grew westward, the affluent population followed. In the 19th century, Society Hill became a community of immigrants along with an African-American community that had been present in the area since colonial times. By the end of the century, the area was dominated by wholesale food markets and poor housing conditions. This led to plans for renewal, which were carried out in the 1960s when the federal urban renewal program allowed historic properties to be acquired for rehabilitation and others to be demolished to make way for new housing.

Society Hill contains a very diverse group of religious properties, including Catholic and Protestant churches, Jewish synagogues, and one of the most significant African-American churches in the country.

The Society Hill tour begins at 3rd Street and Willings Alley, near Walnut Street.

Old St. Paul's Episcopal Church

Episcopal Community Services
3rd Street, between Walnut and Locust streets
1760-61, Robert Smith
1830, remodeled, William Strickland
and Thomas U. Walter
1983-87, adaptive re-use, Dagit/Saylor Associates
Not in currently in religious use.

Open by appointment.
215-351-1400—www.epcs1870.org

Old St. Paul's was founded in 1760 by Reverend William McClenachan whose evangelism and belief in the separation of church and state stirred some of Christ Church's parishioners to form a new congregation. While Christ Church remained a site for British Anglican worship during the Revolutionary War, Old St. Paul's members allied with the colonists. The parish continued to thrive until 1904, when the church became the home of Episcopal Community Services, the human services agency of the Episcopal Diocese of Pennsylvania.

The refined neoclassical facade is a result of the 1830 remodeling by Strickland, one of the most prominent architects of the time, and his assistant, Thomas U. Walter, who would later design the dome of the U.S. Capitol building. The stucco finish is scored to appear like stone, and round-arched windows are filled with clear glass. The sensitive adaptive reuse design of 1987 retained the exterior character as well as the open space, gallery, organ casework and millwork of the interior worship space while accommodating modern offices, meeting rooms and support facilities.

9

10

Old St. Joseph's Roman Catholic Church

Willings Alley, between Walnut & Locust, 3rd and 4th streets
1838-39, John Darragh, master builder
1886, John Deery; 1905, Walter Ballinger & Emile Perrot; 1985, H. Mather Lippincott; 2001, DPK&A; 2006, Milner + Carr Conservation

Services : Sunday: 7:30am, 9:30am, 11am, 6:30pm; Daily Mass: 12:05pm; Saturday: 5:30pm

Open daily for worship.
215-923-1733—www.oldstjoseph.org

Old St. Joseph's was the first Roman Catholic congregation in the city. English Jesuit missionaries erected a small chapel on the site in 1733 and a larger church in 1757. From 1733 until the Revolution, it was the only place in the British Empire where the Catholic mass could legally be offered in public. In the 18th century, Old St. Joseph's cared for Acadian exiles, victims of yellow fever epidemics, refugees from Santo Domingo and thousands of European settlers in a new land. In the 19th century, it became an exemplary urban immigrant parish, responding to the educational and humanitarian needs of thousands of immigrants and African Americans.

The gated courtyard off Willings Alley has been a defining characteristic of this site since the 18th century. Surrounding the courtyard are the 1789 clergy house, the 1839 church and the original St. Joseph's College building of 1851. The church retains the original 1839 Corrie tracker organ and the altar ensemble of Ionic columns surmounted by a carved entablature. The stained glass windows by Alfred Godwin & Co. and ceiling painting by Filippo Costaggini date to the 1886 renovation, which altered much of the interior. Recent restorations have returned the interior to its original colors and character.

Old St. Mary's Roman Catholic Church

4th Street above Spruce Street
1763, builder unknown
1810, 1863, 1886 exterior alterations
1978, interior alterations

Services: Sunday: 10am; Saturday: Vigil, 5pm

Also Open: Monday – Friday: 9:30am – 4:30pm
215-923-7930

The site of Old St. Mary's was established as a Catholic cemetery in 1754. A church was built in 1763 to replace the smaller chapel of Old St. Joseph's. Old St. Mary's became the premier Catholic church of colonial Philadelphia. It was chosen to host the official Prayer Service on July 4, 1779, to observe the anniversary of the Declaration of Independence, with the Founding Fathers in attendance. The churchyard served as the burial site for members of colonial Philadelphia's Catholic community, including heroes of the American Revolution, as well as Catholic foreigners living in Philadelphia. In 1832, a theological training center for future priests was established at Old St. Mary's rectory; it grew to be St. Charles Seminary, now located in Wynnewood.

From 1810 to 1838, Old St. Mary's was the first Cathedral of the Diocese of Philadelphia. This led to a series of alterations that enlarged the church for the growing Catholic population. These included a reorientation of the church, moving the entrance from its original location on the west facade to the east facade and completely reorganizing the interior. In 1978, a significant renovation of the interior, following the reforms of the Second Vatican Council, led to the removal of many historic features.

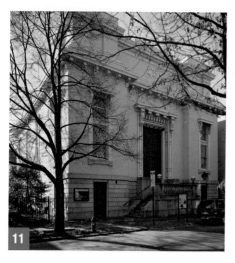

Society Hill Synagogue

Spruce Street, between 4th and 5th streets
1829, 1851, facade, Thomas U. Walter
1985, south extension, James O. Kruhly

*Services: Tuesday: 7:15am; Friday: 8pm;
Saturday: 9:15am*

Open: Monday – Friday: 10am – 3pm

215-922-6590—www.societyhillsynagogue.org

Prominent Philadelphia architect Thomas U. Walter designed this building for his own congregation, the Spruce Street Baptist Church, which worshiped here until 1908. Three years later, the building became the Romanian American Congregation, one of over two dozen ethnic Jewish congregations in the neighborhood. In 1967, the Society Hill synagogue was formed through the union of Romanian and Hungarian American Synagogues, and restoration of the building began.

Walter designed the church in the Greek Revival style with stucco over brick walls scored to look like cut stone. The new congregation made major structural repairs, replaced the roofs, ceiling and windows, rebuilt the towers and restored the facade to Walter's 1851 design by removing twin bell towers that the Romanian congregation had added. Today, the synagogue is a restored community landmark, and the congregation is an active Society Hill institution.

Old Pine Street Presbyterian Church

Pine Street, between 3rd and 4th streets
1766-68, Robert Smith
1857, John Fraser
1951, 1980s restoration; stencils Emily Lapham

*Services: Winter – Sunday: 10:30am;
Summer – Sunday: 9:30am*

Open: Monday – Friday: 9am – 3pm

215-925-8051—www.oldpine.org

Old Pine Street Church, previously named Third Presbyterian Church, is the only colonial Presbyterian church building still standing in Philadelphia. The original building, a simple Georgian-style brick structure, was badly damaged by British troops during the Revolutionary War; it served as a hospital and then as a stable after the pews had been burned for firewood.

In the mid-19th century, the church was remodeled. The interior was divided into two levels with the worship space on the second floor. A Greek Revival-style portico with Corinthian columns was added as well as new windows and the entire building finished in stucco. From 1868 to the 1880s, the ceiling and walls of the sanctuary were decoratively painted with stencils and stained glass windows added.

In 1951, the Friends of Old Pine was established to restore the church. The interior was restored in the 1980s and the stencils recreated in beautiful cream, rose and blue colors. In addition to many Christian symbols, the thistle and wave motifs incorporated into the decoration are reminders of mergers in 1953 and 1959 with the Holland-Scots and the Mariners Presbyterian churches.

Today, the congregation is active in the community; it operates a community center at 4th and Lombard streets and supports a senior housing development in Old City.

St. Peter's Episcopal Church

3rd and Pine streets
1758-61, Robert Smith
1842, tower and spire, William Strickland
Services: Sunday: 9am, 11am, 5pm

Also open: Saturday: 11am – 5pm;
Sunday: 1 – 3pm; weekdays, 9am – 3pm
Inquire at office, 313 Pine Street.

215-925-5968—www.stpetersphila.org

When Christ Church became too crowded and was deemed too far to travel, parishioners living in Society Hill founded St. Peter's in 1757. Thomas and Richard Penn granted land on which to erect a church. St. Peter's shared staff and services with Christ Church until 1832, when the two congregations separated.

Robert Smith's original design for the brick Palladian-style church remains virtually intact today. The exterior has a large two-story east window, marble quoins and round-arched windows. The interior contains box pews, a three-sided gallery and a rococo organ case moved to the east end of the church in 1789. The altar and pulpit are located at opposite ends of the nave. The spire, built by William Strickland, replaced the original frame cupola and remains an important neighborhood landmark.

St. Peter's School, founded in 1834, now independent of the church, abuts the churchyard where many famous Philadelphians are buried. Programs, such as a food cupboard, are run from the parish house on Pine Street.

Kesher Israel Synagogue

Lombard Street, between 4th and 5th streets
1793-95, William Copperthwaite
1895, J. Franklin Stuckert
1991-98 restoration and renovation,
Martin Jay Rosenblum
Services: Friday: 7pm; Saturday: 9am;
Sunday: 8:15am; Monday – Friday: 6:45am

Open by appointment.

215-922-1776

A church was established on this site in 1793 by the First Independent Church of Christ. The building was then occupied by the First Universalist Church in the mid-1800s before it became in 1890 the home of Congregation Kesher Israel, founded by Jewish immigrants from Russia and Eastern Europe. In 1895, the congregation added the Roman brick pavilion, topped by a minaret with a Star of David.

From the exterior, the Star of David in the stained glass windows is the only indication of the synagogue within. However, the atmospheric old-world interior is as decorative as the exterior is austere, A reading platform in the center is lit by antique chandeliers, the ceiling is pressed tin and the walls are decorated with murals painted by Morris Balk in the 1950s. A curved gallery at the second floor lends elegance to the small interior space.

After a period of decline, a rejuvenated congregation completed restoration of the building in 1998, replacing the roof, restoring the daily worship space and making other improvements to enable this distinctive synagogue to continue to serve the Jewish community.

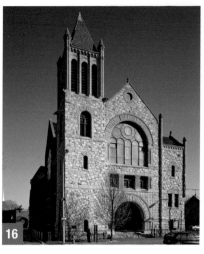

Congregation B'nai Abraham Synagogue

Lombard Street, between 5th and 6th streets
1900-08, Barnet J. Medoff

*Services: Monday – Friday: 7:30am;
Sunday: 8am; Friday evening services at
Vilna Congregation*

Also open by appointment.

215-238-2100—www.phillyshul.com

Founded in 1882, Congregation B'nai Abraham was the first Orthodox congregation in Society Hill. The synagogue is an inspiring structure, designed in the Byzantine-Revival style, a popular alternative to the prevalent Gothic Revival style used for many Christian churches at the time.

However, the synagogue's design may have been a collaboration between Jewish residential and commercial architect Medoff and Charles W. Bolton, a prolific Protestant church designer.

The broad circular stained glass windows, polychromatic facade with raised steps and corner towers that originally supported onion domes create a vivid facade. The interior retains an old-world appearance, with painted wall decoration, a gallery and antique chandeliers. Although the current Orthodox congregation is small, it offers an active religious education program for Jewish youths.

Mother Bethel African Methodist Episcopal Church

6th Street, between Pine and Lombard streets
1889-90, Hazelhurst & Huckel
1997-2007, exterior restoration, Atkin Olshin Lawson-Bell

*Services: Sunday: 8am; 10:45am; Memorial
Day to Labor Day: Sunday: 10am*

*Also open: Tuesday – Friday: 10am – 3pm;
Saturday by appointment.*

215-925-0616—www.motherbethel.org

In 1787, Richard Allen, a freed slave and licensed minister, led fellow blacks away from St. George's Methodist Church in protest of the segregated worship. Allen purchased this site for a new church in 1791. It is believed to be the country's oldest continuously black-owned property in the country. Allen founded the African Methodist Episcopal denomination, of which this is the "mother" church. His tomb and that of his wife, Sarah, along with a small museum are located in the church and open to the public.

The current church, a National Historic Landmark, is the fourth on this site. It is a fine example of the Richardsonian Romanesque style, with broad arches and a square corner tower. While the facade is faced with granite, the rest of the building was finished in brick, a common cost-saving measure. The restored auditorium features opalescent stained glass windows that flood the sanctuary with light, installed in 1890 by the Century Art Company of Philadelphia. The interior is enriched by complex timber framing to support the roof and semicircular pews.

Vilna Congregation (Synagogue)

Pine Street, between 5th and 6th streets
1921, converted to religious use
Services: Friday at sundown; Saturday: 9:30am and at sundown; Sunday: 8am

Also open by appointment.

215-592-9433

The Star of David design in the circular window, and in stained glass over the door and first floor windows, indicates this property, originally a row house, is a Jewish house of worship. Its adaptation into a synagogue probably took place in 1921, when the beige-brick facade with arched windows was added. Row house synagogues, serving a diversity of ethnic congregations, were common in Society Hill and South Philadelphia in the early 1900s.

The worship room on the first floor, with its pressed tin ceiling, provides an intimate space suitable for this small Orthodox congregation. The second floor contains a former women's gallery and meeting room. The notable wall murals may have been painted by the same artist who created murals for Congregation Bínai Abraham and Kesher Israel.

Holy Trinity German Roman Catholic Church

6th and Spruce streets
1788, William Palmer, master builder
Services: Consult Old St. Mary's for schedule.

215-923-7930

Holy Trinity was formed in 1784 at the initiative of German-speaking Catholics who desired to worship and teach their children in their native language. It was the first church erected in the U.S. to serve an ethnic group. It became the precedent for ethnic-oriented parishes formed later in the 19th and 20th centuries to serve and minister to immigrants from Western and Eastern Europe, South and Central America and Asia. In 1797, the parish established America's first Catholic orphanage for children left homeless by yellow fever epidemics.

The church building appears today almost exactly as it did when built in 1789. Sited with the rounded apse, where the altar is located, facing east, the church was originally entered from the west end, through the small churchyard. However, the interior was destroyed by fires in the 1860s and 1890s and again when the roof collapsed in 1995. The current interior reflects a decorative scheme dating from the last fire, with Byzantine and Classical details, American ornamental stained glass windows and an altar painting by Francis Drexel, prominent Philadelphia portrait artist and founder of the Drexel banking business.

Holy Trinity no longer serves as an active parish, but is maintained as an historic site served by Old St. Mary's Church, with Sunday Mass celebrated on a periodic schedule.

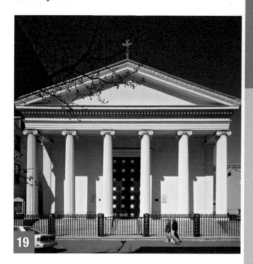

Greek Orthodox Cathedral of St. George

8th Street, between Spruce and Locust streets
1822, John Haviland

Services: Sunday: 9am, 10:30am;
Weekdays: 9:45am

215-627-4389

St. Andrew's Episcopal Church was designed by one of its members, architect John Haviland who was well known for his institutional buildings. It was purchased by St. George's Greek Orthodox congregation in 1922. It was designated a cathedral in 1971.

St. George's retains the high-style Greek Revival exterior of Haviland's design. The facade features six monumental fluted Ionic columns made of wood painted to look like marble. They support a massive entablature decorated with an acanthus frieze and classical details. The church is also constructed of wood covered in stucco scored to look like cut stone.

The interior retains some of the original features including attenuated columns with stylized Egyptian papyrus capitals that support a three-sided gallery decorated with Greek moldings. The ornamental stained glass windows also date from the Episcopal congregation. A fire in the 1930s led to renovations that exposed the roof trusses and incorporate features reflecting Eastern Orthodox worship traditions. The sanctuary is separated from the congregation by a magnificent stenciled and painted altar screen or iconostasis. Icons include Renaissance-styled examples from the 1940s and contemporary Byzantine paintings.

Center Square

Two important religious properties remain in the heart of what is now Philadelphia's retail shopping area. Commercial development grew west along and in Market Street from the market sheds at 2nd Street to a series of outdoor markets as far as 12th Street. These were relocated in the 1850s, creating what is now the Reading Terminal Market beneath the Pennsylvania Convention Center at 12th and Arch streets. In their place came retail stores and major department stores, including the John Wanamaker store near City Hall. Today the area retains this commercial character leaving two historic churches, St. John the Evangelist and St. Stephen's, as sanctuaries within the busy commercial district.

St. Stephen's Church

10th Street, between Market and Chestnut streets
1822-23, William Strickland
1878 transept, Frank Furness
1888 parish house, George C. Mason and Son

Services: Sunday: 10:30am; Thursday: 12pm

Open by appointment.

215-922-3807—www.ststephensphl.org

St. Stephen's is one of the earliest examples of the Gothic Revival style in the country. It is also noteworthy for its exceptional collection of religious art. The exterior reflects Strickland's original design. Its bare granite walls and octagonal crenulated towers are connected by a granite entrance screen with lancet windows. However, the interior has been significantly altered. Nonetheless, the collection of museum-quality ecclesiastical art is what makes St. Stephen's of special interest.

From its founding, St. Stephen's was known for its wealthy, socially prominent parishioners. Many donated works of art and the church deliberately commissioned outstanding works of art to attract congregants. Theses include a collection of exceptional stained glass windows, which date from the second quarter of the 19th century, several Tiffany windows, a pair of English windows by Henry Holiday, and work by D'Ascenzo Studio. Among the memorials is a series by German sculpture Carl Johann Steinhauser commemorating the founder, Edward Shippen Burn, and his children. There is also a Venetian mosaic memorial by Holiday and a marble reredos.

Today St. Stephen's has an active music program, hosts music and theater performances in its sanctuary and has created a performing arts center in its community house.

St. John the Evangelist Roman Catholic Church

13th Street, between Market and Chestnut streets
1831, William Rodrigue
1899, Frank Rushmore Watson

Services (Upper Church): Sunday: 8:30am, 10:30am, 12pm, 6pm; Monday – Friday: 7:45am, 8:30am, 12:05pm, 1:05pm, and 5:15pm; Saturday: 7:45am, 12:05pm, 5:15pm

Open (upper church): Inquire by phone: Monday – Friday: 9am – 5pm.

215-563-5432—www.stjohnsphilly.com

When founded in 1830, St. John's was on the western edge of the expanding city. Its parishioners were prominent families whose fashionable homes were located nearby. As these residences were replaced by office buildings and department stores in the 1900s, St. John's began serving a new weekday congregation of office workers and shoppers.

The parish has a special association with St. John Neumann, Fourth Bishop of Philadelphia who was consecrated in this church in 1852. The graveyard next to the church is the resting place of Thomas Penn Gaskell, the great-great-grandson of William Penn.

The first church was a Gothic design with twin towers. After fire destroyed most of the church in 1899, the remains of the towers were extended and the entire church refaced with rough-faced granite. The entire interior was reconstructed, creating an upper and lower church. Later renovations in 1906 and the 1990s lightened the upper church, creating its current bright interior. Notable elements include the white marble altar and an 1857 marble statue of the Blessed Virgin Mary that survived the fire.

Today the church is operated by the Capuchin Franciscan Friars.

13

Logan Square

Logan Square was known as Northwest Square until 1825. It originally served as a burial ground, and was a place for executions until 1823. The neighborhood around Logan Square began to develop in the mid-19th century as part of the general westward growth of Center City. By the late 19th century the area included both houses and manufacturing facilities. The biggest transformation of the area occurred in the early 20th century with the construction of the Benjamin Franklin Parkway. Over 1,300 buildings were demolished, Logan Square was redesigned, and sites around it were designated for new civic buildings including the Free Library, Franklin Institute and Municipal Courts building. Today the area contains some of the city's most important cultural institutions as well as handsome houses and exceptional examples of Catholic, Episcopal and Quaker religious places that are reminders of the larger residential neighborhood that was here in the 19th century.

The tour of the Logan Square area begins at Broad and Arch streets.

Arch Street United Methodist Church

Arch and Broad streets
1864 chapel, 1868 church, Addison Hutton
1987, restoration
Services: Sunday: 8:30am, 11am: weekdays: in Chapel, 12:15pm

Also open by appointment.

215-568-6250—www.archstreetumc.org

Arch Street United Methodist Church was founded in 1862 to serve an emerging residential neighborhood along North Broad Street. A chapel was built first and then a larger church added, incorporating the chapel into the design. The difference between the old and the new can be readily seen by comparing the rough stone and heavy mortar joints of the chapel to the smooth stone of the church.

The new church was a departure both for the Methodists and the architect, Addison Hutton. Hutton was a Quaker and the simple design of Quaker meetinghouses was similar in character to Wesleyan Methodist churches of the period. But for the new church Hutton selected the Decorated Gothic style and produced a magnificent marble structure with a soaring 233-foot corner tower and spire.

Both the exterior and interior remain true to the original design. In 1987, the auditorium was restored to the original colorful Victorian decorative design, which is complemented by original ornamental stained glass. The 60-foot span is counter-balanced by the balconies, making buttresses and columns unnecessary and creating a wonderful open space. The original organ, while rebuilt several times, is by J.C.B. Standbridge of Philadelphia.

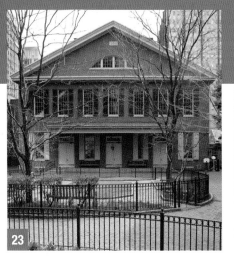

Race Street Meetinghouse

15th and Cherry streets
1856-57, builder unknown
1975, restoration Cope and Lippincott
Services: Sunday: 11am; Summer 10:30am

Open: Inquire at Quaker Information Center, Monday – Friday: 9am – 5pm.

215-241-7024—www.pym.org/philadelphia-qm/central-phila/index.html

Thirty years after the Religious Society of Friends (Quakers) split into two branches, the Hicksite branch constructed a new meetinghouse for their Yearly Meetings. Hicksite Yearly Meetings were held here until 1955 when the two branches reunited and the Yearly Meetings returned to the Arch Street Meetinghouse. One of the distinguishing characteristics of the Hicksite branch was the greater level of participation allowed for women members, among whom were abolitionist Lucretia Mott and peace activist Hannah Clothier Hull. In 1956, the Hicksite monthly meeting united with an Orthodox meeting to form Central Philadelphia Monthly Meeting, which now worships here.

The matching north and south facades are brick with large multi-paned windows, bold cornice and roof moldings and semi-circular windows at the gable ends. The north meeting room retains its historic character; it has a high ceiling accommodating steeply sloped balconies and is furnished with plain wood benches. The south meeting room has been divided into social rooms, offices and classrooms, but retains most original finishes.

The historic building anchors the administrative headquarters of Philadelphia Yearly Meeting and American Friends Service Committee, which are located in the adjacent Friends Center office building.

Living Word Community

La Comunidad Palabra Vivente
17th Street, between Arch and Race streets
c. 1890, architect unknown
Services: Sunday: 10:30am

Open daily.

215-563-1322

The Second Reformed Presbyterian church was founded in 1842 and built a brick church on this site. As the neighborhood grew so did the congregation and a new church was required. It served the congregation until 1922 when the current congregation purchased the building.

The present church reflects the building materials and architectural style popular at the time. The exterior is of brownstone, similar to the facade of the nearby Cathedral of SS. Peter and Paul, with sidewalls of brick. The overall decorative features are in the Gothic Revival style and include quatrefoil moldings, pyramidal caps on the projecting narthex, wood tracery in the pointed arches and trefoil stained glass windows, capped buttresses and pinnacles on the tower. The sanctuary on the second floor retains the original woodwork and original stained glass windows.

The Living Word Community grows out of the Welsh Revival of the early 1900s and places a major focus on racial reconciliation. It has a youth program and a ministry to the homeless community and to others in need.

St. John Chrysostom Albanian Orthodox Church

17th Street, between Race and Vine streets
1847-48, Napoleon LeBrun
Services: Sunday: 10am; Saturday: 6pm
215-563-0979
www.oca.org/DIRlisting.asp?SID=9&KEY=OCA-AL-PHLSJC

The Episcopal Church of the Atonement constructed this church and thrived at this location until the 1890s when the congregation moved to West Philadelphia. It then became Epiphany Chapel and was later occupied by a succession of religious groups. St. John's began worshipping here in the 1930s, ministering to Albanian immigrants. Today, the congregation is composed of descendants of those members as well as recent Albanian immigrants.

The solid granite structure with Gothic details was designed by LeBrun at the same time he was working on the nearby Cathedral of SS. Peter and Paul. While the exterior retains its original cut-stone Gothic character with a prominent carved angel over the entrance doors, the interior has been altered to fit the Orthodox liturgy. A second floor was inserted to provide social space, thereby lowering the ceiling of the nave. Colorful abstract stained glass windows were installed along the side aisles, which are separated from the main seating area by pointed-arch colonnades. Walls are decorated with paintings and murals and, in typical Orthodox form, a painted wood iconostasis separates the sanctuary from the congregation.

Roman Catholic Cathedral Basilica of Saints Peter and Paul

18th Street and Benjamin Franklin Parkway
1846-64, Napoleon LeBrun
1852, facade, John Notman
1914-15, renovations, Henry Dagit
1956-67, renovations, Eggers and Higgins
Services: Sunday: 8am, 9:30, am, 11am, 12:15pm, 5pm; weekdays: 7:15am, 8am, 12:05pm, 12:35pm; Saturday: 12:05pm
Also open: daily 8am–5pm.
215-561-1313
www.archdiocese-phl.org/parishes/7000.htm

By 1844, there were sufficient Catholics in Philadelphia to support the construction of a cathedral, which took 20 years to build. LeBrun, architect for many of the city's Catholic churches in the mid 1800s, conceived the overall plan and design. The magnificent Italian Renaissance-inspired structure is carried out in brownstone and capped by a copper-covered dome, now weathered to a warm green patina. The monumental Corinthian portico was designed by Notman. Construction progressed under Saint John Neumann, Bishop of Philadelphia from 1852 until his death in 1860.

The cathedral has been renovated and modified a number of times during its 150-year history to produce its current sumptuous interior. Decorative elements include murals by Constantino Brumidi (1862), painter of the United States Capitol frescoes; side altars by LeBrun (1877); stained glass windows (1880s); and mosaics (1918, 1957, 1975). The nave is covered by a huge coffered barrel vault. It was extended in 1957 to provide a semicircular apse behind a new altar, which is covered by a domed baldachino.

In 1976, Pope Paul VI designated the cathedral a basilica. Today it is the center of Catholic religious life in Philadelphia.

St. Clement's Church

20th Street, between Cherry and Arch streets
1855-59, John Notman
1897-1933, renovations, Horace Wells Sellers

Services: Sunday: 8am, 10am (June –
September, 11am); Monday & Thursday:
12:10pm; Tuesday, Wednesday, Friday: 7am;
Saturday: 10am

Also open: Monday – Friday: 7am – 12pm
215-563-1876—www.s-clements.org

William Wilson, a speculative housing developer, donated land for an Episcopal church to attract buyers for houses he was building in the immediate area. Notman was both architect and contractor.

The exterior is brownstone in a medieval Romanesque Revival style appropriate for "low" churches of the period. However, starting in the 1870s, the church's clergy and laity were influenced by the Oxford Movement that called for a more Catholic liturgy. They engaged Horace Sellers, a Beaux-Arts trained architect, to renovate the interior. This included a raised floor and ceiling in the chancel, small Gothic windows on the second story and a Lady Chapel with wrought iron gates by Samuel Yellin. The Medieval-style stained glass windows were designed by Charles Connick Studios of Boston in 1940–41.

In 1929, Sellers was responsible for orchestrating the church's move 40 feet to the west when 20th Street was widened as part of the City Beautiful-inspired design for the Benjamin Franklin Parkway. Over three days the 5,500-ton building was moved without causing any damage to the structure. Today, St. Clement's congregation is active in the community and leases part of its parish house to a private school.

Arch Street Presbyterian Church

18th and Arch streets
1853-55, Joseph C. Hoxie

Services: Sunday: 10:45am

Open by appointment.

215-563-3763

Like other churches in the Logan Square area, the West Arch Street Presbyterian Church was founded to serve the rapidly growing neighborhood. The name was changed in 1897 when West Arch merged with another congregation previously located at 10th and Arch streets. In the 1970s, the church merged again, this time with a Welsh Presbyterian church, as a result of which it continues to host special Welsh programs through its relationship with the Welsh Society of Philadelphia.

The church is a mix of architectural styles. The exterior design is based on a Roman Temple. Monumental Corinthian columns support the entablature over the front entrance. Massive piers separate round-arched windows on all sides, and the church is topped by a large copper dome influenced by the design of St. Paul's Cathedral in London. The interior is one of the finest religious interiors in the city. Skylights brighten the Classical Revival-style sanctuary, which contains heavy Baroque ornamentation and a pedimented podium, all covered by a coffered dome and ceiling. The upholstered box pews seat 1,100 people.

Today Arch Street Presbyterian remains a special oasis in an area dominated by the city's tallest buildings.

Rittenhouse Square

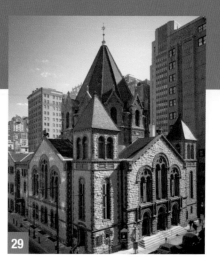

29

I n the late 19th century, wealthy families decided to skip over the vacant land west of Broad Street to build elegant mansions in the area around Rittenhouse Square, one of the original four squares set aside by William Penn. Speculative developers followed and built large Victorian row houses, which were in turn followed by the construction of large churches. Today the area around Rittenhouse Square is one of the city's finest residential neighborhoods and most distinctive historic districts. It contains exceptional examples of 19th-century row houses, including many of the best brownstones in the city.

Rittenhouse Square itself is an important meeting place and the location of outdoor art exhibits, concerts and a variety of public events.

Within a short walking distance of the square are a number of outstanding religious buildings designed by the most prominent architects of their time including John Notman, John McArthur, Jr. (architect of City Hall) and Frank Furness.

The tour of the Rittenhouse Square area begins at 17th and Sansom streets.

First Baptist Church

17th and Sansom streets
1900, Edgar Viguers Seeler
Services: Sunday: 11am; Wednesday: 12pm
Also open daily: 12 – 2pm.
215-563-3853—www.fbcphila1698.org

The first Baptist congregation was founded in 1698 in Old City. Several churches were built there, but as that neighborhood changed and the more affluent population moved west new churches were built first at Broad and Arch streets in 1856 and then at the present location in 1898. First Baptist is considered a "mother" church, and from its ranks nearly a dozen congregations had their beginnings.

The church is a delightful mix of Byzantine and Romanesque styles. The Romanesque exterior is of polychromatic grey granite and pink sandstone with rounded arches and carved stone details. Inside, a colorful dome that gives the church its Byzantine character covers a Greek-cross plan. Stained glass windows with solemn, stately figures, designed by Heinike and Bowen of New York, surround the large sanctuary.

Today the congregation shares its building with many educational, community, art, self-help and human services organizations.

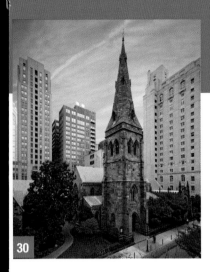

St. Mark's Episcopal Church

Locust Street, between 16th and 17th streets
1847-52, John Notman
1900-02, Lady Chapel, Cope and Stewardson

*Services: Sunday: 8:30am – 11am; Monday –
Friday: 7:30am – 8:30am, 12:10pm – 5:30pm;
Saturday: 10am*

215-735-1416

www.saintmarksphiladelphia.org

The founders of St. Mark's were influenced
by the 19th-century Anglican reform movement, which advocated correct medieval
Gothic Revival design for church buildings.
On the exterior, the church appears to be a
group of buildings, reflecting the independent expression of different elements. The
interior follows the medieval practice of leaving all construction materials in their natural
condition. Hammer-dressed stonewalls and
ceilings and oak trusses support a slate roof.
Except for a single 16th-century panel, all
windows are of a Victorian design, represent-
ing important 19th-century English, German
and Philadelphia studios. Other notable features are the iron hinges by Samuel Yellin on
the entrance doors, the choir woodwork by
Henry Vaughan and the chancel railing and
pulpit by Ralph Adams Cram.

Rich embellishments from generous
donors appeared between 1890 and 1925.
The most impressive are the groin-vaulted
Lady Chapel and the silver-encased altar,
both donated by Rodman Wanamaker.

In addition to hosting a variety of music
performances, the congregation provides
social programs as well as meeting space for
community organizations.

Tenth Presbyterian Church

17th and Spruce streets
1855-1857, John McArthur, Jr.
1893, interior renovations, Frank Miles Day

Services: Sunday: 9am, 11am, 6:30pm

*Also open: weekdays 9am – 5:30pm
(enter at 1701 Delancey Street).*

215-735-7688—www.tenth.org

By 1852, the population of the area west of
Broad Street had grown so rapidly that the
Tenth Presbyterian Church sponsored a new
West Spruce Street Presbyterian Church. In
1892, the two churches merged into a single
congregation at this location.

John McArthur, Jr., architect of City
Hall, was deacon of the church and thus had
a special interest in the building's design. The
church's eclectic architecture borrows from
many styles: the Italianate-style brick exterior
contains Romanesque rounded arches, windows and pilasters and originally had an
extraordinary French Gothic 250-foot-tall
spire that was removed in 1912. The interior
retains a Byzantine-inspired decorative
scheme installed in the 1890s when the two
congregations merged. It includes two stained
glass windows from Tiffany Studios, "Angel
in a Field of Lilies" and an ornamental window with the Presbyterian Coat of Arms.

Today Tenth Presbyterian is one of the
largest Center City Presbyterian congregations. Its ministries include global outreach
and relief work, outreach to homeless, a
children's choir, a free public concert series, a
Christian bookstore (open Sunday), a college-
preparatory school, and broadcast and
Webcast services.

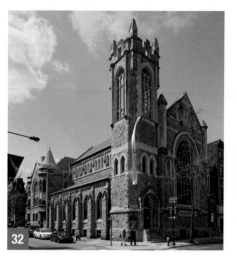

Temple Beth Zion-Beth Israel

18th and Spruce streets
1894, Thomas Preston Lonsdale
1954, conversion to synagogue, Beryl Price

*Services: Monday – Friday: 7:45am, 5:30pm;
Friday: 7pm; Saturday and Sunday: 9am*

*Also open: Monday – Thursday: 9am – 5pm;
Friday: 9am – 3pm.*

215-735-5148—www.bzbi.org

This outstanding neo-Gothic church was
originally the Covenant United Methodist
Church. It was converted into a synagogue
in 1954. The present congregation represents
the merger of three Conservative synagogues.
The oldest, Temple Beth Israel, was founded
in 1840 by German and Polish immigrants.
It merged in 1964 with the 18-year-old
Temple Beth Zion to serve a revitalized
Jewish community. In 1984, the Nezinger
Synagogue, founded in 1889 by Eastern
European Jews, merged into the
congregation.

A fine time to enjoy this building is after
dark, when the jewel-toned stained glass
windows are lit from within. They depict the
first five books of the Bible, the Torah, and
are a collaborative creation of architect Price
and stained glass craftsman Vincent Filipone.
The windows' unique design restrains the
building's Gothic style by emphasizing
horizontal lines and spreading color across
the windows.

The main sanctuary is notable for its
gold-veiled Great Ark that stands before a
cathedral-height raw silk curtain. These features and fine mosaics, reliefs and woodcarv-
ings were designed by architect Price in
collaboration with various artists.

First Church of Christ, Scientist

Pine Street, between 19th and 20th streets
c. 1874-77, James Peacock Sims
1892, porch and alterations, Frank Furness

Services: Sunday: 11am; Wednesday: 7:30pm

Open by appointment.

215-545-2899

This small chapel, with its long side parallel
to the street, was constructed under the aus-
pices of Christ Church as outreach to the
growing Rittenhouse Square neighborhood.
Only a portion of the building was completed because of limited funds, with plans to
finish the structure as membership grew. In
1930, the building was sold to Fifth Church
of Christ, Scientist, now First Church of
Christ, Scientist.

The exterior uses terra cotta for ornamentation, the first use of this material docu-
mented in Philadelphia. Victorian Gothic-
style influences are notable in the steeply
pitched roof and most especially in the polychromatic wall treatment, where red and
black brick contrast with pale stone window
surrounds. Although the exterior remains
unchanged, the interior has been modified in
keeping with Christian Science services.

The unadorned interior consists of white
painted stonewalls and a dark wood ceiling
supported by exposed trusses. The 13 original
memorial windows, some of them by Tiffany,
were removed when the church ceased to be
an Episcopal church. Their replacement with
leaded glass allowed more light into the
church and contributes to its simple
character.

The church sponsors a Christian Science
Reading Room at 1935 Chestnut Street and a
weekly Saturday morning radio program.

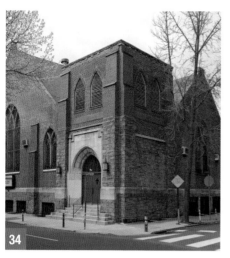

34

35

New Central Baptist Church

Lombard Street at Van Pelt Street, between 21st and 22nd streets
1925, J. Erle Druckenmiller
1943, supervised by Reverend August Havershare
Services: Sunday: 10:45am

215-732-4267

The African-American congregation of New Central Baptist Church created a one-story church building in 1925. This is visible in the corner pavilions and stone base of the current church. The second floor brick structure was added under the leadership of Reverend August Havershare, the dynamic pastor of the church from 1942 to 1979.

The second floor sanctuary has a truncated cross plan with the altar, choir and baptismal areas along the long side, thereby providing an intimate setting for the congregation. The interior is brightly lit by large stained glass windows, including a large circular window over the choir loft. The first floor is now used for social functions and religious education.

Trinity Memorial Church, Episcopal

22nd and Spruce streets
1874-75, James Peacock Sims
1994-97, renovations and restoration, Atkin Olshin Lawson-Bell
Services: Sunday: 10:30am

Open: Inquire by phone, Tuesday – Friday: 2:30 – 6:30pm.

215-732-2515—www.trinityphiladelphia.org

Trinity Chapel was erected as a memorial and served as a chapel until 1948 when the congregation became independent. The Gothic style exterior is of brownstone, with two towers, a high nave and low side aisles. The interior features a hammer-beam truss and an increasingly rare set of American-made Victorian ornamental stained-glass windows, probably installed at the time the church was built. Unique to the design are the iron buttresses that brace the exterior wall and allow natural light to pass through the clerestory windows while keeping the interior column-free.

A disastrous fire in 1994 destroyed the church roof and gutted most of the interior. The parish took this opportunity to completely reconfigure the sanctuary so that it could be used for many functions, including concerts, conferences and meetings as well as church services. Today an independent non-profit, Trinity Center for Urban Life, manages the buildings for the benefit of the neighborhood. The church sponsors many social programs including a Community OutReach Partnership, which manages the Wintershelter for homeless men. The parish house is also home to Trinity Playgroup, a daycare center.

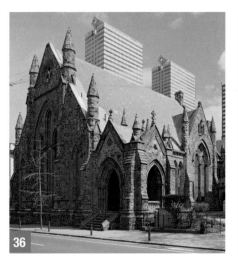

Church of the New Jerusalem

22nd and Chestnut streets
1881-83, 1908, angel staircase, Theophilus
Parsons Chandler, Jr.
1989, renovation, Mark B. Thompson

Not currently in religious use.

Open by appointment only.

215-279-9999—www.cfi-knoll.com

The Swedenborgian denomination built its
first church in Philadelphia in 1816 and
a second in the mid-19th century. Both
were sold, one to a Unitarian church, and
this site was purchased for a new church in
1881. However, 100 years later the congregation had grown too small to maintain the
church. Working closely with preservation
organizations, the congregation sold the
church, which was sensitively adapted for
private offices.

The church was one of the most prominent commissions of Theophilus Parson
Chandler, founder and administrator of
the School of Architecture at the University
of Pennsylvania. Chandler chose the early
English Gothic style for the church and
parish house, both of which are executed
in brownstone and retain their original
appearance.

The interior was altered to insert three
floors of offices into the nave in a manner
that allowed the chancel area to be visible
and the altar, pulpit and some original furniture to be preserved. In 2005, the church was
purchased by Corporate Facilities, Inc., a
supplier of high-end commercial furniture to
large corporate clients.

First Unitarian Church

Chestnut Street, between 21st and 22nd streets
1883-86, Furness, Evans and Company
1921, tower altered, 1955, facade altered, R.
Brognard Okie

Service: Sunday: 11am

*Also open: Monday – Friday: 8am – 6pm;
Sunday: 10am – 1pm.*

215-563-3980—www.firstuu-philly.org

The Society of Unitarian Christians was
formed in Philadelphia in 1796. It prospered
and grew under the leadership of Reverend
William Henry Furness who served as pastor
for 50 years. When the church decided to
erect a new building in the fashionable
Rittenhouse Square area, they selected Rev.
Furness's son as architect. First Unitarian is
notable as the only Center City church
designed in its entirety by Frank Furness, one
of Philadelphia's great architects of the 19th
century. It is a fine example of his eccentric
style.

The exterior has been greatly altered from
the original design with the removal of the
porte-cochere and tower. However, the interi-
or retains its original character with great
hammer-beam trusses, oak pews and Furness-
designed furniture. The original color scheme
of cerulean blue walls and rust red ceiling
stenciled with gold-leaf daffodils has been
restored after having been painted over in the
1920s. Among the church's significant
stained glass windows, some by Tiffany
Studios, are memorials to members of the
Furness family by the English artist Henry
Holiday.

Today First Unitarian draws its congregation from across the Delaware Valley and
provides space for youth, human services
programs, public forums and musical
performances.

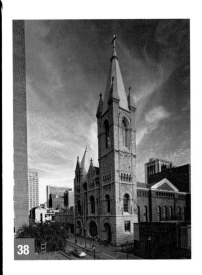

Lutheran Church of the Holy Communion

Chestnut Street between 21st and 22nd streets
1879-80, Isaac Pursell

Services: Sunday: 9am, 11am

Also open: Inquire by phone.
Monday – Friday: 10am – 4pm.

215-567-3668

www.lutheranchurchphiladelphia.org

Like other dominations, Lutherans moved to establish new churches west of Broad Street in the late 19th century. Their first location was at Broad and Arch Streets, then in 1903, they purchased St. Paul's Reformed Episcopal Church.

Holy Communion's sandstone exterior and five-story tower dominate Chestnut Street. The broad round arches over the portals and windows indicate the Richardsonian Romanesque style and give the facade a monumental quality. The original Episcopalian congregation saved money by finishing the sidewalls in brick. Inside the auditorium is an expansive open space with Classical piers and moldings.

In 1905, Holy Communion's congregants removed the original second floor gallery and inserted the pulpit, baptismal font, organ and panel altar from their previous church at Broad and Arch streets. The opalescent and ornamental windows along the sidewalls of the sanctuary allow an abundance of colorful light into the space, as does the Tiffany window inserted into the original carved wood reredos.

Holy Communion allows community organizations to use its church and the Stevens Community Center for meetings, performances and other functions and continues to serve by its motto: "In the City for Good."

First Presbyterian Church

21st and Walnut streets
1869-72, Henry Augustus Sims
1900, tower, Frank Furness
1953, interior renovations

Services: Sunday: 11am

Also open: Monday – Friday: 9am – 5pm.

215-567-0532 —phpwebsite.fpcphila.org

When construction began in 1869, the church was located in a quickly developing section of the city. It housed the Second Presbyterian congregation, a group that had split from the First Presbyterian Church in 1743. The two reunited in worship in this structure in 1949.

This High Victorian Gothic-style treasure is enriched by the works of many talented artisans. It was designed by Sims, a civil engineer whose brother was a notable church architect. Furness, Philadelphia's great late-19th-century architect, designed the asymmetrical corner tower. Inside are many significant stained glass windows ranging from work by 19th-century Philadelphia craftsmen and the Tiffany Studios, to windows imported from England and Belgium. Polished marble nave column capitals were carved by Alexander Milne Calder, who was responsible for the sculpture on City Hall.

Today, the congregation participates in a broad range of ministries to children, and to the elderly, the sick and the homeless.

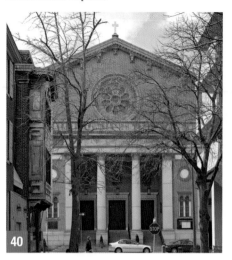

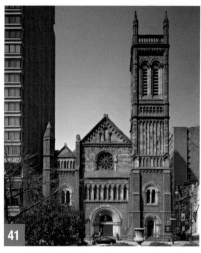

St. Patrick's Roman Catholic Church

20th Street, between Locust and Spruce streets
1910-1917, Ballinger & Perrot

Services: Sunday: 8am. 10am, 12pm, 6:30pm, Saturday: 9am; Weekdays: 7:30am, 12:05pm

Open daily for worship.

215-735-9900

www.archdiocese-phl.org/parishes/8305.htm

This Catholic parish's long and colorful history began with its founding in 1839 as a place of worship for Irish immigrants working at nearby coal wharves on the Schuylkill River. Its first building was erected in 1841 and survived the 1844 anti-Catholic riots when guards were posted nearby. The congregation grew rapidly in the late 1800s, leading to the construction of the present church. The neo-Classical structure was fitted to its site by cutting off planned transept arms and constructing a raised worship space above a full-size chapel, which contains the church's original altar. The large sanctuary with exposed brick walls seats 1,200. It has a Byzantine plan capped by a broad Guastavino tile dome. Windows from Munich, designed to recall French Gothic stained glass, and a tile floor complete the impressive interior. The mosaic Stations of the Cross were designed by Nicholas Thouran in 1955.

Church of the Holy Trinity, Rittenhouse Square

19th and Walnut streets
1856-59, John Notman
1868, tower, John Fraser
1880, renovations, Henry Van Brunt and James Peacock Sims

Services: Sunday: 8:30am, 11am; Tuesday and Friday: 8:30am; Tuesday and Thursday: 12:15pm

Open by appointment.

215-567-1267—www.htrit.org

Holy Trinity is one of the oldest structures on Rittenhouse Square. It is one of the first and finest examples of the Norman Romanesque Revival style in the country. The exterior, sheathed in warm-colored brownstone, exhibits the round arches and corbelling that define the style. The prominent corner tower is a Walnut Street landmark.

Inside, Holy Trinity's rich variety of decorative finishes and memorial stained glass windows are indicative of the wealthy, but less conservative, members of a Low Episcopalian Church. English, French and American stained glass studios are represented, including Philadelphia artist William Willet, who received national acclaim when his window was installed here in 1917. Also notable are the murals on the expansive barrel-vaulted ceiling and the rose window on the facade. Holy Trinity was home to Phillip Brooks, the rector during the Civil War, who wrote the words to "O Little Town of Bethlehem," with music by organist Lewis Redner. As a result, in 1924, muralist Hildreth Meiere was commissioned to paint scenes of the nativity on the chancel apse walls.

The church hosts many musical and theatrical performances and also provides space for meetings, workshops and educational activities for a variety of human services and community organizations.

South Broad Street

B road Street was designated as the major north-south street in William Penn's plan, but the city grew west very slowly and development did not begin along Broad Street until after 1840. Originally it was the site of fashionable residential mansions and cultural institutions such as the Academy of Music. However, the construction of City Hall on Center Square beginning in 1868 attracted commercial uses to the area south of City Hall. By the early 20th century, many of the city's major hotels, banks and office buildings were located along South Broad Street, most of which remain.

At the end of the 20th century, Broad Street was designated as the Avenue of the Arts, and major performance facilities were constructed south of Locust Street, including the Kimmel Center for the Performing Arts. Today South Broad Street is a mix of offices, hotels, restaurants, theaters and concert halls. The few religious properties in the area reflect the presence of residential neighborhoods to the east and west.

The South Broad Street tour begins at Broad and Pine streets.

Chambers-Wylie Memorial Presbyterian Church
Broad Street Ministry
Broad Street, between Spruce and Pine streets
1899-1900, Rankin & Kellogg
Services: Sunday: 6pm
215-917-2251—www.broadstreetministry.org

This Gothic Revival church was constructed for the Wylie Presbyterian Church and named for its first pastor, Reverend Samuel Wylie. Wylie Memorial later merged with the Chambers Presbyterian Church, of which department store founder John Wanamaker was a member. As Broad Street became more commercial, the congregation declined and the church was vacant for many years before the Broad Street Ministry was formed in 2005.

The church has a refined Gothic appearance with thin lancet windows, a triple portal and twin crenellated towers. Its balanced and elegant design is a result, no doubt, of Rankin & Kellogg's experience in designing institutional buildings with Beaux-Arts finesse.

Broad Street Ministry offers non-traditional services that include a wide variety of forms of worship from music to meditation. It reaches out to the arts community and the diverse population of the adjacent neighborhoods, seeking to provide a place where spiritual questing meets artistic expression. In addition, the church houses a variety of other programs, including the dance program of the University of the Arts.

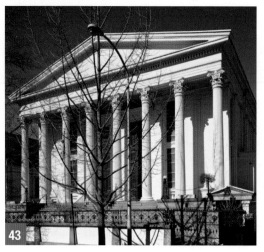

The Church of St. Luke and the Epiphany (Episcopal)

13th Street, between Pine and Spruce streets
1839-40, Thomas S. Stewart
1874, parish house, Furness & Hewitt
Services: Sunday: 9am, 11am; Summer: 10am

Open by appointment.

215-732-1918

www.stlukeandtheepephany.org

This stately late Greek Revival church was originally home to St. Luke's Church, founded in 1839 to serve a rapidly growing residential neighborhood. It merged with the Church of The Epiphany in 1898.

St. Luke and the Epiphany is one of the most important early-19th-century Greek Revival churches. The giant Corinthian-column portico stands on a raised platform set behind a fine stucco and wrought-iron fence. The interior is equally impressive. Corinthian columns frame a circular chancel.

Corinthian pilasters, balconies faced with acanthus moldings and Greek fretwork, and a coffered ceiling complete the handsome interior decoration. The adjacent parish house, designed by architect Frank Furness, was restored in the 1990s in the spirit of its original color scheme.

St. Luke and the Epiphany has long been recognized as both a spiritual home and a community center. Activities include cultural performances, social outreach to the homeless, neighborhood and condo association meetings and social gatherings. The church is highly regarded for its outreach to the gay community. The weekly services of Dignity Philadelphia are held here.

St. Peter Claver Roman Catholic Church

St. Peter Claver Center for Evangelization

12th and Lombard streets
1841, Thomas Ustick Walter
Not currently in religious use.

Open for tours and information.

215-735-3164

While African-American Catholics in Philadelphia can trace their records to the early 1700s, it was not until 1886 that they formed the St. Peter Claver Union. The group was named in honor of a 16th-century Spanish priest who devoted his life to the service of African slaves. In 1892, the church was dedicated as the Mother Church for Black Catholics in the Archdiocese of Philadelphia. It served as a Catholic parish and school until it was closed in 1985. In 1995, it became the St. Peter Claver Center for Evangelization. The purpose of the center is education, outreach and preservation of the history of Black Catholics. The fine neo-Classical church is notable for its symmetrical appearance, triple-portal, Doric pilasters and classical moldings. Inside, the church features a pair of rare windows by French designer Louis Koch. Wealthy Philadelphian and later Saint Katharine Drexel and Father Augustine Tolton, the first recognized African-American Catholic priest in the United States, both worshiped at this church.

First Tabernacle Beth El Church of God and Saints of Christ (Jewish)

Broad and South streets
1886, Charles M. Burns
Services: Friday: 7pm; Saturday: 9am

This English Gothic-inspired church was originally constructed for an Episcopal parish, the Church of Ascension, which was one of the most important in the Pennsylvania Diocese in the 1920s when it was known as the Pro-Cathedral Church of St. Mary. Since 1956, the church has been home to First Tabernacle Beth El, an African-American Hebrew congregation that worships in a traditional Jewish manner.

The building retains its original exterior appearance. Many of the notable interior features, such as the stained glass windows in the nave and chancel that depict unusual Biblical scenes, have been retained. However, the sanctuary has been remodeled to serve its function as a synagogue.

Wesley African Methodist Episcopal Zion Church

15th and Lombard streets
1924, George Savage
Services: Sunday: 10:45am

Open by appointment.

215-735-8961

The First Colored Wesley Methodist Church separated from Mother Bethel A.M.E. Church in 1820 and purchased an existing brick church on this site in 1885. The congregation later commissioned a larger structure from George Savage, who designed a granite Gothic Revival church with a prominent corner tower and pointed-arch windows with tracery. The spire was removed after a 1942 storm. A large sanctuary on the second floor has large galleries on either side and a beamed ceiling and is lit on all four sides by stained glass windows.

Wesley's active congregation has been a historical leader in the development of the African Methodist Episcopal (A.M.E.) Zion denomination, and was a leader in the civil rights and social reform movements in the 1950s and 1960s.

The following two churches are no longer in religious use and are not open to the public.

St. Andrew's Ukrainian Catholic Church

Pine Street, between 4th and 5th streets
Society Hill

St. Andrew's is a modest yellow-brick structure that features three copper-clad bulbous domes. Originally a Jewish educational center, the building was purchased and modified for use as a church by an immigrant Ukrainian/Slavic congregation from 1944 to 1952. The building is currently vacant.

St. Philip's Episcopal Church

Lombard Street, between 19th and 20th streets
Rittenhouse Square

This modest Gothic-style brick building was purchased by Holy Trinity Church as a Sunday school and chapel for the area's African-American population. It was named for Philips Brooks, Holy Trinity's rector. In 1954, the chapel became an independent congregation serving a primarily West Indian congregation. Today it is occupied by a daycare center.

Index by denomination

Credits
Project coordinator and research: Elizabeth Blazevich
Editing: Elise Vider
Design: Willie • Fetchko Graphic Design
Photography: All photographs © 2007 Tom Crane, except cover lower right and buildings number 2 and 6 © 2007 Wyatt Gallery